THE ELDER STATESMAN

By T. S. Eliot

COMPLETE POEMS AND PLAYS OF T. S. ELIOT

verse

COLLECTED POEMS, 1909–1962
THE WASTE LAND
THE WASTE LAND: A FACSIMILE AND TRANSCRIPT
(Edited by Valerie Eliot)
FOUR QUARTETS
POEMS WRITTEN IN EARLY YOUTH

selected verse

SELECTED POEMS

children's verse

OLD POSSUM'S BOOK OF PRACTICAL CATS
THE ILLUSTRATED OLD POSSUM

plays

COLLECTED PLAYS
MURDER IN THE CATHEDRAL
THE FAMILY REUNION
THE COCKTAIL PARTY
THE CONFIDENTIAL CLERK
THE ELDER STATESMAN

selected prose

SELECTED PROSE OF T. S. ELIOT
(Edited with an introduction by Frank Kermode)

literary criticism

SELECTED ESSAYS
THE USE OF POETRY *and* THE USE OF CRITICISM
ON POETRY AND POETS
FOR LANCELOT ANDREWES

social criticism

NOTES TOWARDS THE DEFINITION OF CULTURE

philosophy

KNOWLEDGE AND EXPERIENCE
in the philosophy of F. H. Bradley

THE ELDER STATESMAN

T. S. Eliot

FABER AND FABER
London · Boston

First published in 1969
by Faber and Faber Limited
3 Queen Square London WC1
First published in Faber Paperbacks 1973
Reprinted 1976 and 1980
Printed in Great Britain by
Whitstable Litho Ltd Whitstable Kent

ISBN 0 571 10274 3

TO MY WIFE

To whom I owe the leaping delight
That quickens my senses in our wakingtime
And the rhythm that governs the repose of our sleepingtime,
    The breathing in unison

Of lovers . . .
Who think the same thoughts without need of speech
And babble the same speech without need of meaning:

To you I dedicate this book, to return as best I can
With words a little part of what you have given me.
The words mean what they say, but some have a further meaning
    For you and me only.

ERRATUM

Page 59 Last 4 lines should read:

It is through this meeting that I shall at last escape them.
I've made my confessions to you, Monica:
That is the first step taken towards my freedom,
And perhaps the most important. I know what you think.

The Cast of the First Production
at the
Edinburgh Festival
August 25–August 30 1958

Monica Claverton-Ferry	ANNA MASSEY
Charles Hemington	RICHARD GALE
Lambert	GEOFFREY KERR
Lord Claverton	PAUL ROGERS
Federico Gomez	WILLIAM SQUIRE
Mrs. Piggott	DOROTHEA PHILLIPS
Mrs. Carghill	EILEEN PEEL
Michael Claverton-Ferry	ALEC McCOWEN

Presented by HENRY SHEREK
Directed by E. MARTIN BROWNE
Settings designed by HUTCHINSON SCOTT

Characters

Monica Claverton-Ferry
Charles Hemington
Lambert
Lord Claverton
Federico Gomez
Mrs. Piggott
Mrs. Carghill
Michael Claverton-Ferry

ACT ONE

The drawing-room of Lord Claverton's London house. Four o'clock in the afternoon

ACT TWO

The Terrace at Badgley Court. Morning

ACT THREE

The Same. Late afternoon of the following day

Act One

The drawing-room of LORD CLAVERTON'S *London house. Four o'clock in the afternoon.*

[*Voices in the hall*]

CHARLES. Is your father at home to-day?

MONICA.   You'll see him at tea.

CHARLES. But if I'm not going to have you to myself
There's really no point in my staying to tea.

[*Enter* MONICA *and* CHARLES *carrying parcels*]

MONICA. But you *must* stay to tea. That was understood
When you said you could give me the whole afternoon.

CHARLES. But I couldn't say what I wanted to say to you
Over luncheon . . .

MONICA.   That's your own fault.
You should have taken me to some other restaurant
Instead of to one where the *maître d'hôtel*
And the waiters all seem to be your intimate friends.

CHARLES. It's the only place where I'm really well known
And get well served. And when *you're* with me
It must be a perfect lunch.

MONICA.   It was a perfect lunch.
But I know what men are — they like to show off.
That's masculine vanity, to want to have the waiters
All buzzing round you: and it reminds the girl
That she's not the only one who's been there with him.

CHARLES. Well, tease me if you like. But a man does feel a fool
If he takes you to a place where he's utterly unknown
And the waiters all appear to be avoiding his eye.

MONICA. We're getting off the point . . .

CHARLES.   You've got me off *my* point . . .
I was trying to explain . . .

MONICA.   It's simply the question
Of your staying to tea. As you practically promised.

CHARLES. What you don't understand is that I have a grievance.

On Monday you're leaving London, with your father:
I arranged to be free for the whole afternoon
On the plain understanding . . .

MONICA.   That you should stop to tea.

CHARLES. When I said that I was free for the whole afternoon,
That meant you were to give *me* the whole afternoon.
I couldn't say what I wanted to, in a restaurant;
And then you took me on a shopping expedition . . .

MONICA. If you don't like shopping with me . . .

CHARLES.   Of course I like shopping with you.
But how can one *talk* on a shopping expedition —
Except to guess what you want to buy
And advise you to buy it.

MONICA.   But why not stop to tea?

CHARLES. Very well then, I will stop to tea,
But you know I won't get a chance to talk to you.
You know that. Now that your father's retired
He's at home every day. And you're leaving London.
And because your father simply can't bear it
That any man but he should have you to himself,
Before I've said two words he'll come ambling in . . .

MONICA. You've said a good deal more than two words already.
And besides, my father doesn't amble.
You're not at all respectful.

CHARLES.   I try to be respectful;
But you know that I shan't have a minute alone with you.

MONICA. You've already had several minutes alone with me
Which you've wasted in wrangling. But seriously, Charles,
Father's sure to be buried in the library
And he won't think of leaving it until he's called for tea.
So why not talk now? Though I know very well
What it is you want to say. I've heard it all before.

CHARLES. And you'll hear it again. You think I'm going to tell you
Once more, that I'm in love with you. Well, you're right.
But I've something else to say that I haven't said before,
That will give you a shock. I believe *you* love *me*.

MONICA. Oh, what a dominating man you are!
Really, you must imagine you're a hypnotist.

CHARLES. Is this a time to torment me? But I'm selfish
In saying that, because I think —

I think you're tormenting yourself as well.

MONICA. You're right. I am. Because *I am* in love with you.

CHARLES. So I was right! The moment I'd said it
  I was badly frightened. For I didn't *know* you loved me —
  I merely wanted to believe it. And I've made you say so!
  But now that you've said so, you must say it again,
  For I need so much assurance! Are you sure you're not mistaken?

MONICA. How did this come, Charles? It crept so softly
  On silent feet, and stood behind my back
  Quietly, a long time, a long long time
  Before I felt its presence.

CHARLES.   Your words seem to come
  From very far away. Yet very near. You are changing me
  And I am changing you.

MONICA.   Already
  How much of me is you?

CHARLES.   And how much of me is you?
  I'm not the same person as a moment ago.
  What do the words mean now — *I* and *you*?

MONICA. In our private world — now we have our private world —
  The meanings are different. Look! We're back in the room
  That we entered only a few minutes ago.
  Here's an armchair, there's the table;
  There's the door . . . and I hear someone coming:
  It's Lambert with the tea . . .
  [*Enter* LAMBERT *with trolley*]
                              and I shall say, 'Lambert,
  Please let his lordship know that tea is waiting'.

LAMBERT. Yes, Miss Monica.

MONICA.   I'm very glad, Charles,
  That you *can* stay to tea.

                                    [*Exit* LAMBERT]
                    — Now we're in the public world.

CHARLES. And your father will come. With his calm possessive air
  And his kindly welcome, which is always a reminder
  That I mustn't stay too long, for you belong to him.
  He seems so placidly to take it for granted
  That you don't really care for any company but his!

MONICA. You're not to assume that anything I've said to you
  Has given you the right to criticise my father.

13

In the first place, you don't understand him;
In the second place, we're not engaged yet.

CHARLES. Aren't we? We're agreed that we're in love with each other,
And, there being no legal impediment
Isn't that enough to constitute an engagement?
Aren't you sure that you want to marry me?

MONICA. Yes, Charles. I'm sure that I want to marry you
When I'm free to do so. But by that time
You may have changed your mind. Such things have happened.

CHARLES. That won't happen to me.

[*Knock. Enter* LAMBERT]

LAMBERT. Excuse me, Miss Monica. His Lordship said to tell you
Not to wait tea for him.

MONICA.   Thank you, Lambert.

LAMBERT. He's busy at the moment. But he won't be very long.

[*Exit*]

CHARLES. Don't you understand that you're torturing me?
How long will you be imprisoned, alone with your father
In that very expensive hotel for convalescents
To which you're taking him? And what after that?

MONICA. There are several good reasons why I should go with
    him.

CHARLES. Better reasons than for marrying me?
What reasons?

MONICA.   First, his terror of being alone.
In the life he's led, he's never had to be alone.
And when he's been at home in the evening,
Even when he's reading, or busy with his papers
He needs to have someone else in the room with him,
Reading too — or just sitting — someone
Not occupied with anything that can't be interrupted.
Someone to make a remark to now and then.
And mostly it's been me.

CHARLES.   I know it's been you.
It's a pity that you haven't had brothers and sisters
To share the burden. Sisters, I should say,
For your brother's never been of any use to you.

MONICA. And never will be of any use to anybody,
I'm afraid. Poor Michael! Mother spoilt him
And Father was too severe — so they're always at loggerheads.

CHARLES. But you spoke of several reasons for your going with your
    father.
    Is there any better reason than his fear of solitude?
MONICA. The second reason is exactly the opposite:
    It's his fear of being exposed to strangers.
CHARLES. But he's most alive when he's among people
    Managing, manœuvring, cajoling or bullying —
    At all of which he's a master. Strangers!
MONICA. You don't understand. It's one thing meeting people
    When you're in authority, with authority's costume,
    When the man that people see when they meet you
    Is not the private man, but the public personage.
    In politics Father wore a public label.
    And later, as chairman of public companies,
    Always his privacy has been preserved.
CHARLES. His privacy has been so well preserved
    That I've sometimes wondered whether there was any . . .
    Private self to preserve.
MONICA.   There *is* a private self, Charles.
    I'm sure of that.
CHARLES.   You've given two reasons,
    One the contradiction of the other.
    Can there be a third?
MONICA.   The third reason is this:
    I've only just been given it by Dr. Selby —
    Father is much iller than he is aware of:
    It may be, he will never return from Badgley Court.
    But Selby wants him to have every encouragement —
    If he's hopeful, he's likely to live a little longer.
    That's why Selby chose the place. A *convalescent* home
    With the atmosphere of an hotel —
    Nothing about it to suggest the clinic —
    Everything about it to suggest recovery.
CHARLES. This is your best reason, and the most depressing;
    For this situation may persist for a long time,
    And you'll go on postponing and postponing our marriage.
MONICA. I'm afraid . . . not a very long time, Charles.
    It's almost certain that the winter in Jamaica
    Will never take place. 'Make the reservations'
    Selby said, 'as if you were going'.

But Badgley Court's so near your constituency!
You can come down at weekends, even when the House is sitting.
And you can take me out, if Father can spare me.
But he'll simply love having you to talk to!

CHARLES. I know he's used to seeing me about.

MONICA. I've seen him looking at you. He was thinking of himself
When he was your age — when he started like you,
With the same hopes, the same ambitions —
And of his disappointments.

CHARLES.   Is that wistfulness,
Compassion, or . . . envy?

MONICA.   Envy is everywhere.
Who is without envy? And most people
Are unaware or unashamed of being envious.
It's all we can ask if compassion and wistfulness . . .
And tenderness, Charles! are mixed with envy:
I do believe that he is fond of you.
So you must come often. And Oh, Charles dear —

[*Enter* LORD CLAVERTON]

MONICA. You've been very long in coming, Father. What have you been
doing?

LORD CLAVERTON. Good afternoon, Charles. You might have guessed,
Monica,
What I've been doing. Don't you recognise this book?

MONICA. It's your engagement book.

LORD CLAVERTON.   Yes, I've been brooding over it.

MONICA. But what a time for your engagement book!
You know what the doctors said: complete relaxation
And to think about nothing. Though I know that won't be easy.

LORD CLAVERTON. That is just what I was doing.

MONICA.   Thinking of nothing?

LORD CLAVERTON. Contemplating nothingness. Just remember:
Every day, year after year, over my breakfast,
I have looked at this book — or one just like it —
You know I keep the old ones on a shelf together;
I could look in the right book, and find out what I was doing
Twenty years ago, to-day, at this hour of the afternoon.
If I've been looking at this engagement book, to-day,
Not over breakfast, but before tea,
It's the empty pages that I've been fingering —

The first empty pages since I entered Parliament.
I used to jot down notes of what I had to say to people:
Now I've no more to say, and no one to say it to.
I've been wondering . . . how many more empty pages?

MONICA. You would soon fill them up if we allowed you to!
That's my business to prevent. You know I'm to protect you
From your own restless energy — the inexhaustible
Sources of the power that wears out the machine.

LORD CLAVERTON. They've dried up, Monica, and you know it.
They talk of rest, these doctors, Charles; they tell me to be cautious,
To take life easily. Take life easily!
It's like telling a man he mustn't run for trains
When the last thing he wants is to take a train for anywhere!
No, I've not the slightest longing for the life I've left —
Only fear of the emptiness before me.
If I had the energy to work myself to death
How gladly would I face death! But waiting, simply waiting,
With no desire to act, yet a loathing of inaction.
A fear of the vacuum, and no desire to fill it.
It's just like sitting in an empty waiting room
In a railway station on a branch line,
After the last train, after all the other passengers
Have left, and the booking office is closed
And the porters have gone. What am I waiting for
In a cold and empty room before an empty grate?
For no one. For nothing.

MONICA.   Yet you've been looking forward
To this very time! You know how you grumbled
At the farewell banquet, with the tributes from the staff,
The presentation, and the speech you had to make
And the speeches that you had to listen to!

LORD CLAVERTON [pointing to a silver salver, still lying in its case].
        I don't know which impressed me more, the insincerity
Of what was said about me, or of my reply —
All to thank them for that.
                              Oh the grudging contributions
That bought this piece of silver! The inadequate levy
That made the Chairman's Price! And my fellow directors
Saying 'we must put our hands in our pockets
To double this collection — it must be something showy'.

This would do for visiting cards — if people still left cards
And if I was going to have any visitors.

MONICA. Father, you simply want to revel in gloom!
You know you've retired in a blaze of glory —
You've read every word about you in the papers.

CHARLES. And the leading articles saying 'we are confident
That his sagacious counsel will long continue
To be at the disposal of the Government in power'.
And the expectation that your voice will be heard
In debate in the Upper House . . .

LORD CLAVERTON.   The established liturgy
Of the Press on any conspicuous retirement.
My obituary, if I had died in harness,
Would have occupied a column and a half
With an inset, a portrait taken twenty years ago.
In five years' time, it will be the half of that;
In ten years' time, a paragraph.

CHARLES.   That's the reward
Of every public man.

LORD CLAVERTON.   Say rather, the exequies
Of the failed successes, the successful failures,
Who occupy positions that other men covet.
When we go, a good many folk are mildly grieved,
And our closest associates, the small minority
Of those who really understand the place we filled
Are inwardly delighted. They won't want my ghost
Walking in the City or sitting in the Lords.
And I, who recognise myself as a ghost
Shan't want to be seen there. It makes me smile
To think that men should be frightened of ghosts.
If they only knew how frightened a ghost can be of men!

[*Knock. Enter* LAMBERT]

LAMBERT. Excuse me, my Lord. There's a gentleman downstairs
Is very insistent that he must see you.
I told him you never saw anyone, my Lord,
But by previous appointment. He said he knew that,
So he had brought this note. He said that when you read it
You would want to see him. Said you'd be very angry
If you heard that he'd gone away without your seeing him.

LORD CLAVERTON. What sort of a person?

LAMBERT. A foreign person
By the looks of him. But talks good English.
A pleasant-spoken gentleman.

LORD CLAVERTON [*after reading the note*]. I'll see him in the library.
No, stop. I've left too many papers about there.
I'd better see him here.

LAMBERT. Very good, my Lord.
Shall I take the trolley, Miss Monica?

MONICA. Yes, thank you, Lambert.

[*Exit* LAMBERT]

CHARLES. I ought to be going.

MONICA. Let *us* go into the library. And then I'll see you off.

LORD CLAVERTON. I'm sorry to turn you out of the room like this,
But I'll have to see this man by myself, Monica.
I've never heard of this Señor Gomez
But he comes with a letter of introduction
From a man I used to know. I can't refuse to see him.
Though from what I remember of the man who introduces him
I expect he wants money. Or to sell me something worthless.

MONICA. You ought not to bother with such people now, Father.
If you haven't got rid of him in twenty minutes
I'll send Lambert to tell you that you have to take a trunk call.
Come, Charles. Will you bring my coat?

CHARLES. I'll say goodbye, sir.
And look forward to seeing you both at Badgley Court
In a week or two.

[*Enter* LAMBERT]

LAMBERT. Mr. Gomez, my Lord.

LORD CLAVERTON. Goodbye, Charles. And please remember
That we both want to see you, whenever you can come
If you're in the vicinity. Don't we, Monica?

MONICA. Yes, Father. (*To* CHARLES) We *both* want to see you.

[*Exeunt* MONICA *and* CHARLES]

[LAMBERT *shows in* GOMEZ]

LORD CLAVERTON. Good evening, Mr. . . . . Gomez. You're a friend of
Mr. Culverwell?

GOMEZ. We're as thick as thieves, you might almost say.
Don't you know me, Dick?

LORD CLAVERTON. Fred Culverwell!
Why do you come back with another name?

GOMEZ. You've changed your name too, since I knew you.
    When we were up at Oxford, you were plain Dick Ferry.
    Then, when you married, you took your wife's name
    And became Mr. Richard Claverton-Ferry;
    And finally, Lord Claverton. I've followed your example,
    And done the same, in a modest way.
    You know, where *I* live, people do change their names;
    And besides, my wife's name is a good deal more normal
    In my country, than Culverwell — and easier to pronounce.

LORD CLAVERTON. Have you lived out there ever since . . . you left
    England?

GOMEZ. Ever since I finished my sentence.

LORD CLAVERTON. What has brought you to England?

GOMEZ.   Call it homesickness,
    Curiosity, restlessness, whatever you like.
    But I've been a pretty hard worker all these years
    And I thought, now's the time to take a long holiday,
    Let's say a rest cure — that's what I've come for.
    You see, I'm a widower, like you, Dick.
    So I'm pretty footloose. Gomez, you see,
    Is now a highly respected citizen
    Of a central American republic: San Marco.
    It's as hard to become a respected citizen
    Out there, as it is here. With this qualification:
    Out there they respect you for rather different reasons.

LORD CLAVERTON. Do you mean that you've won respect out
    there
    By the sort of activity that lost you respect
    Here in England?

GOMEZ.   Not at all, not at all.
    I think that was rather an unkind suggestion.
    I've always kept on the right side of the law —
    And seen that the law turned its right side to *me*.
    Sometimes I've had to pay pretty heavily;
    But I learnt by experience whom to pay;
    And a little money laid out in the right manner
    In the right places, pays many times over.
    I assure you it does.

LORD CLAVERTON.   In other words
    You have been engaged in systematic corruption.

GOMEZ. No, Dick, there's a fault in your logic.
How can one corrupt those who are already corrupted?
I can swear that I've never corrupted anybody.
In fact, I've never come across an official
Innocent enough to be corruptible.

LORD CLAVERTON. It would seem then that most of your business
Has been of such a nature that, if carried on in England,
It might land you in gaol again?

GOMEZ.   That's true enough,
Except for a false inference. I wouldn't dream
Of carrying on such business if I lived in England.
I have the same standards of morality
As the society in which I find myself.
I do nothing in England that you would disapprove of.

LORD CLAVERTON. That's something, at least, to be thankful for.
I trust you've no need to engage in forgery.

GOMEZ. Forgery, Dick? An absurd suggestion!
Forgery, I can tell you, is a mug's game.
I say that — with conviction.
No, forgery, or washing cheques, or anything of that nature,
Is certain to be found out sooner or later.
And then what happens? You have to move on.
That wouldn't do for me. I'm too domestic.
And by the way, I've several children,
All grown up, doing well for themselves.
I wouldn't allow either of my sons
To go into politics. In my country, Dick,
Politicians can't afford mistakes. The prudent ones
Always have an aeroplane ready:
And keep an account in a bank in Switzerland.
The ones who don't get out in time
Find themselves in gaol and not very comfortable,
Or before a firing squad.
You don't know what serious politics is like!
I said to my boys: 'Never touch politics.
Stay out of politics, and play both parties:
What you don't get from one you may get from the other'.
Dick, don't tell me that there isn't any whisky in the house?

LORD CLAVERTON. I can provide whisky. [*Presses the bell*]
                          But why have you come?

GOMEZ. You've asked me that already!
    To see you, Dick. A natural desire!
    For you're the only old friend I can trust.
LORD CLAVERTON. You really trust me? I appreciate the compliment.
GOMEZ. Which you're sure you deserve. But when I say 'trust' . . .
[*Knock. Enter* LAMBERT]
LORD CLAVERTON. Lambert, will you bring in the whisky. And soda.
LAMBERT. Very good, my Lord.
GOMEZ.   And some ice.
LAMBERT. Ice? Yes, my Lord.

                                                            [*Exit*]

GOMEZ. I began to say: when I say 'trust'
    I use the term as experience has taught me.
    It's nonsense to talk of trusting people
    In general. What does that mean? One trusts a man
    Or a woman — in this respect or that.
    A won't let me down in this relationship,
    B won't let me down in some other connection.
    But, as I've always said to my boys:
    'When you come to the point where you need to trust someone
    You must make it worth his while to be trustworthy'.
        [*During this* LAMBERT *enters silently, deposits tray and exit*]
LORD CLAVERTON. Won't you help yourself?
                [GOMEZ *does so, liberally*]
GOMEZ.   And what about you?
LORD CLAVERTON. I don't take it, thank you.
GOMEZ.   A reformed character!
LORD CLAVERTON. I should like to know why you need to trust *me*.
GOMEZ. That's perfectly simple. I come back to England
    After thirty-five years. Can you imagine
    What it would be like to have been away from home
    For thirty-five years? I was twenty-five —
    The same age as you — when I went away,
    Thousands of miles away, to another climate,
    To another language, other standards of behaviour,
    To fabricate for myself another personality
    And to take another name. Think what that means —
    To take another name.
            [*Gets up and helps himself to whisky*]
                    But of course you know!

Just enough to think you know more than you do.
You've changed your name twice — by easy stages,
And each step was merely a step up the ladder,
So you weren't aware of becoming a different person:
But where *I* changed my name, there was no social ladder.
It was jumping a gap — and you can't jump back again.
I parted from myself by a sudden effort,
You, so slowly and sweetly, that you've never woken up
To the fact that Dick Ferry died long ago.
I married a girl who didn't know a word of English,
Didn't want to learn English, wasn't interested
In anything that happened four thousand miles away,
Only believed what the parish priest told her.
I made my children learn English — it's useful;
I always talk to them in English.
But do they think in English? No, they do not.
They think in Spanish, but their thoughts are Indian thoughts.
O God, Dick, *you* don't know what it's like
To be so cut off! Homesickness!
Homesickness is a sickly word.
You don't understand such isolation
As mine, you think you do . . .

LORD CLAVERTON.　　　　　　I'm sure I do,
　　I've always been alone.

GOMEZ.　　　　　　　　Oh, loneliness —
　　Everybody knows what that's like.
　　Your loneliness — so cosy, warm and padded:
　　You're not isolated — merely insulated.
　　It's only when you come to see that you have lost *yourself*
　　That you are quite alone.

LORD CLAVERTON.　　　　I'm waiting to hear
　　Why you should need to trust me.

GOMEZ.　　　　　　　Perfectly simple.
　　My father's dead long since — that's a good thing.
　　My mother — I dare say she's still alive,
　　But she must be very old. And she must think I'm dead;
　　And as for my married sisters — I don't suppose their husbands
　　Were ever told the story. *They* wouldn't want to see me.
　　No, I need one old friend, a friend whom I can trust —
　　And one who will accept both Culverwell and Gomez —

    See Culverwell as Gomez — Gomez as Culverwell.
    I need you, Dick, to give me reality!

LORD CLAVERTON. But according to the description you have given
    Of trusting people, how do you propose
    To make it **worth my** while to be trustworthy?

GOMEZ. It's done **already**, Dick; done many years ago:
    Adoption **tried, and** grappled to my soul
    With hoops of steel, and all that sort of thing.
    We'll come to that, very soon. Isn't it strange
    That there should always have been this bond between us?

LORD CLAVERTON. It has never crossed my mind. Develop the point.

GOMEZ. Well, consider what we were when we went up to Oxford
    And then what I became under your influence.

LORD CLAVERTON. You cannot attribute your . . . misfortune to *my*
    influence.

GOMEZ. I was just about as different as anyone could be
    From the sort of men you'd been at school with —
    I didn't fit into your set, and I knew it.
    When you started to take me up at Oxford
    I've no doubt your friends wondered what you found in me —
    A scholarship boy from an unknown grammar school.
    I didn't know either, but I was flattered.
    Later, I came to understand: you made friends with me
    Because it flattered *you* — tickled your love of power
    To see that I was flattered, and that I admired you.
    Everyone expected that I should get a First.
    I suppose your tutor thought you'd be sent down.
    It went the other way. You stayed the course, at least.
    I had plenty of time to think things over, later.

LORD CLAVERTON. And what is the conclusion that you came to?

GOMEZ. This is how it worked out, Dick. You liked to play the rake,
    But you never went too far. There's a prudent devil
    Inside you, Dick. He never came to *my* help.

LORD CLAVERTON. I certainly admit no responsibility,
    None whatever, for what happened to you later.

GOMEZ. You led me on at Oxford, and left me to it.
    And so it came about that I was sent down
    With the consequences which you remember:
    A miserable clerkship — which your father found for me,
    And expensive tastes — which you had fostered in me,

And, equally unfortunate, a talent for penmanship.
Hence, as you have just reminded me
Defalcation and forgery. And then my stretch
Which gave me time to think it all out.

LORD CLAVERTON. That's the second time you have mentioned your
reflections.
But there's just one thing you seem to have forgotten:
I came to your assistance when you were released.

GOMEZ. Yes, and paid my passage out. I know the reason:
You wanted to get rid of me. I shall tell you why presently.
Now let's look for a moment at *your* life history.
You had plenty of money, and you made a good marriage —
Or so it seemed — and with your father's money
And your wife's family influence, you got on in politics.
Shall we say that you did very well by yourself?
Though not, I suspect, as well as you had hoped.

LORD CLAVERTON. I was never accused of making a mistake.

GOMEZ. No, in England mistakes are anonymous
Because the man who accepts responsibility
Isn't the man who made the mistake.
That's your convention. Or if it's known you made it
You simply get moved to another post
Where at least you can't make quite the same mistake.
At the worst, you go into opposition
And let the other people make mistakes
Until your own have been more or less forgotten.
I dare say you did make some mistake, Dick . . .
That would account for your leaving politics
And taking a conspicuous job in the City
Where the Government could always consult you
But of course didn't have to take your advice . . .
I've made a point, you see, of following your career.

LORD CLAVERTON. I am touched by your interest.

GOMEZ.   I have a gift for friendship.
I rejoiced in your success. But one thing has puzzled me.
You were given a ministry before you were fifty:
That should have led you to the very top!
And yet you withdrew from the world of politics
And went into the City. Director of a bank
And chairman of companies. You looked the part —

Cut out to be an impressive figurehead.
But again, you've retired at sixty. Why at sixty?

LORD CLAVERTON. Knowing as much about me as you do
You must have read that I retired at the insistence of my doctors.

GOMEZ. Oh yes, the usual euphemism.
And yet I wonder. It *is* surprising:
You should have been good for another five years
At least. Why did they let you retire?

LORD CLAVERTON. If you want to know, I had had a stroke.
And I might have another.

GOMEZ.   Yes. You might have another.
But I wonder what brought about this . . . stroke;
And I wonder whether you're the great economist
And financial wizard that you're supposed to be.
And I've learned something of other vicissitudes.
Dick, I was very very sorry when I heard
That your marriage had not been altogether happy.
And as for your son — from what I've heard about *him*,
He's followed your undergraduate career
Without the protection of that prudent devil
Of yours, to tell him not to go too far.
Well, now, I'm beginning to be thirsty again.

[*Pours himself whisky*]

LORD CLAVERTON. An interesting historical epitome.
Though I cannot accept it as altogether accurate.
The only thing I find surprising
In the respected citizen of San Marco
Is that in the midst of the engrossing business
Of the nature of which dark hints have been given,
He's informed himself so carefully about my career.

GOMEZ. I don't propose to give you a detailed account
Of my own career. I've been very successful.
What would have happened to me, I wonder,
If I had never met you? I should have got my First,
And I might have become the history master
In a school like that from which I went to Oxford.
As it is, I'm somebody — a more important man
In San Marco than I should ever have been in England.

LORD CLAVERTON. So, as you consider yourself a success . . .

GOMEZ. A worldly success, Dick. In another sense

We're both of us failures. But even so,
I'd rather be my kind of failure than yours.

LORD CLAVERTON. And what do you call failure?

GOMEZ.   What do I call failure?
The worst kind of failure, in my opinion,
Is the man who has to keep on pretending to himself
That he's a success — the man who in the morning
Has to make up his face before he looks in the mirror.

LORD CLAVERTON. Isn't that the kind of pretence that you're
        maintaining
In trying to persuade me of your . . . worldly success?

GOMEZ. No, because I know the value of the coinage
I pay myself in.

LORD CLAVERTON. Indeed! How interesting!
I still don't know why you've come to see me
Or what you mean by saying you can trust me.

GOMEZ. Dick, do you remember the moonlight night
We drove back to Oxford? *You* were driving.

LORD CLAVERTON. That happened several times.

GOMEZ.   One time in particular.
You know quite well to which occasion I'm referring —
A summer night of moonlight and shadows —
The night you ran over the old man in the road.

LORD CLAVERTON. You *said* I ran over an old man in the road.

GOMEZ. You knew it too. If you had been surprised
When I said 'Dick, you've run over somebody'
Wouldn't you have shown it, if only for a second?
You never lifted your foot from the accelerator.

LORD CLAVERTON. We were in a hurry.

GOMEZ.   More than in a hurry.
You didn't want it to be known where we'd been.
The girls who were with us (what were their names?
I've completely forgotten them) you didn't want *them*
To be called to give evidence. You just couldn't face it.
Do you see now, Dick, why I say I can trust you?

LORD CLAVERTON. If you think that this story would interest the
        public
Why not sell your version to a Sunday newspaper?

GOMEZ. My dear Dick, what a preposterous suggestion!
Who's going to accept the unsupported statement

Of Federico Gomez of San Marco
About something that happened so many years ago?
What damages you'd get! The Press wouldn't look at it.
Besides, you can't think I've any desire
To appear in public as Frederick Culverwell?
No, Dick, your secret's safe with me.
Of course, I might give it to a few friends, in confidence.
It might even reach the ears of some of your acquaintance —
But you'd never know to whom I'd told it,
Or who knew the story and who didn't. I promise you.
Rely upon me as the soul of discretion.

LORD CLAVERTON. What do you want then? Do you need money?

GOMEZ. My dear chap, you are obtuse!
I said: 'Your secret is safe with me',
And then you . . . well, I'd never have believed
That you would accuse an old friend of . . . blackmail!
On the contrary, I dare say I could buy you out
Several times over. San Marco's a good place
To make money in — though not to *keep* it in.
My investments — not all in my own name either —
Are pretty well spread. For the matter of that,
My current account in Stockholm or Zürich
Would keep me in comfort for the rest of my life.
Really, Dick, you owe me an apology.
Blackmail! On the contrary
Any time you're in a tight corner
My entire resources are at your disposal.
You were a generous friend to me once
As you pointedly reminded me a moment ago.
Now it's my turn, perhaps, to do you a kindness.

[*Enter* LAMBERT]

LAMBERT. Excuse me, my Lord, but Miss Monica asked me
To remind you there's a trunk call coming through for you
In five minutes' time.

LORD CLAVERTON.   I'll be ready to take it.

[*Exit* LAMBERT]

GOMEZ. Ah, the pre-arranged interruption
To terminate the unwelcome intrusion
Of the visitor in financial distress.
Well, I shan't keep you long, though I dare say your caller

Could hang on for another quarter of an hour.

LORD CLAVERTON. Before you go — what is it that you want?

GOMEZ. I've been trying to make clear that I only want your friendship!
Just as it used to be in the old days
When you taught me expensive tastes. Now it's my turn.
I can have cigars sent direct to you from Cuba
If your doctors allow you a smoke now and then.
I'm a lonely man, Dick, with a craving for affection.
All I want is as much of your company,
So long as I stay here, as I can get.
And the more I get, the longer I may stay.

LORD CLAVERTON.   This is preposterous!
Do you call it friendship to impose your company
On a man by threats? Why keep up the pretence?

GOMEZ. Threats, Dick! How can you speak of threats?
It's most unkind of you. My only aim
Is to renew our friendship. Don't you understand?

LORD CLAVERTON. I see that when I gave you my friendship
So many years ago, I only gained in return
Your envy, spite and hatred. That is why you attribute
Your downfall to me. But how was I responsible?
We were the same age. You were a free moral agent.
You pretend that I taught you expensive tastes:
If you had not had those tastes already
You would hardly have welcomed my companionship.

GOMEZ. Neatly argued, and almost convincing:
Don't you wish you could believe it?

LORD CLAVERTON.   And what if I decline
To give you the pleasure of my company?

GOMEZ. Oh, I can wait, Dick. You'll relent at last.
You'll come to feel easier when I'm with you
Than when I'm out of sight. You'll be afraid of whispers,
The reflection in the mirror of the face behind you,
The ambiguous smile, the distant salutation,
The sudden silence when you enter the smoking room.
                              Don't forget, Dick:
You *didn't stop*! Well, I'd better be going.
I hope I haven't outstayed my welcome?
Your telephone pal may be getting impatient.
I'll see you soon again.

LORD CLAVERTON.   Not very soon, I think.

   I am going away.

GOMEZ.   So I've been informed.

   I have friends in the press — if not in the peerage.

   Goodbye for the present. It's been an elixir

   To see you again, and assure myself

   That we can begin just where we left off.

[*Exit* GOMEZ]

[LORD CLAVERTON *sits for a few minutes brooding. A knock. Enter*
MONICA.]

MONICA. Who was it, Father?

LORD CLAVERTON.   A man I used to know.

MONICA. Oh, so you knew him?

LORD CLAVERTON.   Yes. He'd changed his name.

MONICA. Then I suppose he wanted money?

LORD CLAVERTON.   No, he didn't want money.

MONICA. Father, this interview has worn you out.

   You must go and rest now, before dinner.

LORD CLAVERTON. Yes, I'll go and rest now. I wish Charles was
        dining with us.

   I wish we were having a dinner party.

MONICA. Father, can't you bear to be alone with me?

   If you can't bear to dine alone with me tonight,

   What will it be like at Badgley Court?

CURTAIN

Act Two

The terrace of Badgley Court. A bright sunny morning, several days later.
Enter LORD CLAVERTON *and* MONICA.

MONICA. Well, so far, it's better than you expected,
    Isn't it, Father? They've let us alone;
    The people in the dining-room show no curiosity;
    The beds are comfortable, the hot water is hot,
    They give us a very tolerable breakfast;
    And the chambermaid really *is* a chambermaid:
    For when I asked about morning coffee
    She said 'I'm not the one for elevens's,
    That's Nurse's business'.
LORD CLAVERTON.   So far, so good.
    I'll feel more confidence after a fortnight —
    After fourteen days of people not staring
    Or offering picture papers, or wanting a fourth at bridge;
    Still, I'll admit to a feeling of contentment
    Already. I only hope that it will last —
    The sense of wellbeing! It's often with us
    When we are young, but then it's not noticed;
    And by the time one has grown to consciousness
    It comes less often.
                I hope this benignant sunshine
    And warmth will last for a few days more.
    But this early summer, that's hardly seasonable,
    Is so often a harbinger of frost on the fruit trees.
MONICA. Oh, let's make the most of this weather while it lasts.
    I never remember you as other than occupied
    With anxieties from which you were longing to escape;
    Now I want to see you learning to enjoy yourself!
LORD CLAVERTON. Perhaps I've never really enjoyed living
    As much as most people. At least, as they seem to do
    Without knowing that they enjoy it. Whereas I've often known

That I didn't enjoy it. Some dissatisfaction
With myself, I suspect, very deep within myself
Has impelled me all my life to find justification
Not so much to the world — first of all to myself.
What is this self inside us, this silent observer,
Severe and speechless critic, who can terrorise us
And urge us on to futile activity,
And in the end, judge us still more severely
For the errors into which his own reproaches drove us?

MONICA. You admit that at the moment you find life pleasant,
That it really does seem quiet here and restful.
Even the matron, though she looks rather dominating,
Has left us alone.

LORD CLAVERTON. Yes, but remember
What she said. She said: 'I'm going to leave you alone!
You want perfect peace: that's what Badgley Court is for.'
I thought that very ominous. When people talk like that
It indicates a latent desire to interfere
With the privacy of others, which is certain to explode.

MONICA. Hush, Father. I see her coming from the house.
Take your newspaper and start reading to me.

[*Enter* MRS. PIGGOTT]

MRS. PIGGOTT. Good morning, Lord Claverton! Good morning, Miss
Claverton!
Isn't this a glorious morning!
I'm afraid you'll think I've been neglecting you;
So I've come to apologise and explain.
I've been in such a rush, these last few days,
And I thought, 'Lord Claverton will understand
My not coming in directly after breakfast:
He's led a busy life, too.' But I hope you're happy?
Is there anything you need that hasn't been provided?
All you have to do is to make your wants known.
Just ring through to my office. If I'm not there
My secretary will be — Miss Timmins.
She'd be overjoyed to have the privilege of helping you!

MONICA. You're very kind . . . Oh, I'm sorry,
We don't know how we ought to address you.
Do we call you 'Matron'?

MRS. PIGGOTT.   Oh no, not 'Matron'!

Of course, I *am* a matron in a sense —
No, I don't simply mean that I'm a married woman —
A widow in fact. But I was a Trained Nurse,
And of course I've always lived in what you might call
A medical milieu. My father was a specialist
In pharmacology. And my husband
Was a distinguished surgeon. Do you know, I fell in love with him
During an appendicitis operation!
I was a theatre nurse. But you mustn't call me 'Matron'
At Badgley Court. You see, we've studied to avoid
Anything like a nursing-home atmosphere.
We don't want our guests to think of themselves as ill,
Though we never have guests who are perfectly well —
Except when they come like you, Miss Claverton.

MONICA. Claverton-Ferry. Or Ferry: it's shorter.

MRS. PIGGOTT. So sorry. Miss Claverton-Ferry. I'm Mrs. Piggott.
Just call me Mrs. Piggott. It's a short and simple name
And easy to remember. But, as I was saying,
Guests in perfect health are exceptional
Though we never accept any guest who's incurable.
You know, we've been deluged with applications
From people who want to come here to die!
We never accept them. Nor do we accept
Any guest who *looks* incurable —
We make that stipulation to all the doctors
Who send people here. When you go in to lunch
Just take a glance around the dining-room:
Nobody looks ill! They're all convalescents,
Or resting, like you. So you'll remember
Always to call me Mrs. Piggott, won't you?

MONICA. Yes, Mrs. Piggott, but please tell me one thing.
We haven't seen her yet, but the chambermaid
Referred to a nurse. When we see her
Do we address her as 'Nurse'?

MRS. PIGGOTT.   Oh yes, that's different.
She is a real nurse, you know, fully qualified.
Our system is very delicately balanced:
For me to be simply 'Mrs. Piggott'
Reassures the guests in one respect;
And calling our nurses 'Nurse' reassures them

    In another respect.

LORD CLAVERTON.   I follow you perfectly.

MRS. PIGGOTT. And now I must fly. I've so much on my hands!
    But before I go, just let me tuck you up . . .
    You must be very careful at this time of year;
    This early warm weather can be very treacherous.
    There, now you look more comfy. Don't let him stay out late
    In the afternoon, Miss Claverton-Ferry.
    And remember, when you want to be *very* quiet
    There's the Silence Room. With a television set.
    It's popular in the evenings. But not *too* crowded.

                                                 [*Exit*]

LORD CLAVERTON. Much as I had feared. But I'm not going to say
    Nothing could be worse. Where there's a Mrs. Piggott
    There may be, among the guests, something worse than Mrs.
        Piggott.

MONICA. Let's hope this was merely the concoction
    Which she decants for every newcomer.
    Perhaps after what she considers proper courtesies,
    She will leave us alone.

[*Re-enter* MRS. PIGGOTT]

MRS. PIGGOTT.   I really *am* neglectful!
    Miss Claverton-Ferry, I ought to tell you more
    About the amenities which Badgley Court
    Can offer to guests of the younger generation.
    When there are enough young people among us
    We dance in the evening. At the moment there's no dancing,
    And it's still too early for the bathing pool.
    But several of our guests are keen on tennis,
    And of course there's always croquet. But I don't advise croquet
    Until you know enough about the other guests
    To know whom *not* to play with. I'll mention no names,
    But there are one or two who don't like being beaten,
    And that spoils any sport, in my opinion.

MONICA. Thank you, Mrs. Piggott. But I'm very fond of walking
    And I'm told there are very good walks in this neighbourhood.

MRS. PIGGOTT. There are indeed. I can lend you a map.
    There are lovely walks, on the shore or in the hills,
    Quite away from the motor roads. You must learn the best walks.
    I won't apologise for the lack of excitement:

After all, peace and quiet is our *raison d'être*.
Now I'll leave you to enjoy it.

[*Exit*]

MONICA. I hope she won't remember anything else.
LORD CLAVERTON. She'll come back to tell us more about the peace
        and quiet.
MONICA. I don't believe she'll be bothering us again:
    I could see from her expression when she left
    That she thought she'd done her duty by us for to-day.
    I'm going to prowl about the grounds. Don't look so alarmed!
    If you spy any guest who seems to be stalking you
    Put your newspaper over your face
    And pretend you're pretending to be asleep.
    If they think you *are* asleep they'll do something to wake you,
    But if they see you're shamming they'll have to take the hint.

[*Exit*]

A moment later, LORD CLAVERTON *spreads his newspaper over his face.*
    Enter MRS. CARGHILL. *She sits in a deckchair nearby, composes*
    herself and takes out her knitting.
MRS. CARGHILL [*after a pause*]. I hope I'm not disturbing you. I
        always sit here.
    It's the sunniest and most sheltered corner,
    And none of the other guests have discovered it.
    It was clever of you to find it so quickly.
    What made you choose it?
LORD CLAVERTON [*throwing down newspaper*]. My daughter chose it.
    She noticed that it seemed to offer the advantages
    Which you have just mentioned. I am glad you can confirm them.
MRS. CARGHILL. Oh, so that *is* your daughter — that very charming
        girl?
    And obviously devoted to her father.
    I was watching you both in the dining-room last night.
    You are the great Lord Claverton, aren't you?
    Somebody said you were coming here —
    It's been the topic of conversation.
    But I couldn't believe that it would really happen!
    And now I'm sitting here talking to you.
    Dear me, it's astonishing, after all these years;
    And you don't even recognise me! I'd know you anywhere.
    But then, we've all seen your portrait in the papers

So often. And everybody knows *you*. But still,
I wish you could have paid *me* that compliment, Richard.

LORD CLAVERTON. What!

MRS. CARGHILL.   Don't you know me yet?

LORD CLAVERTON.   I'm afraid not.

MRS. CARGHILL. There were the three of us — Effie, Maudie and me.
That day we spent on the river — I've never forgotten it —
The turning point of all my life!
Now whatever were the names of those friends of yours
And which one was it invited us to lunch?
I declare, I've utterly forgotten their names.
And you gave us lunch — I've forgotten what hotel —
But such a good lunch — and we all went in a punt
On the river — and we had a tea basket
With some lovely little cakes — I've forgotten what you called them,
And you made me try to punt, and I got soaking wet
And nearly dropped the punt pole, and you all laughed at me.
Don't you remember?

LORD CLAVERTON.   Pray continue.
The more you remind me of, the better I'll remember.

MRS. CARGHILL. And the three of us talked you over afterwards —
Effie and Maud and I. What a time ago it seems!
It's surprising I remember it all so clearly.
You attracted me, you know, at the very first meeting —
I can't think why, but it's the way things happen.
I said 'there's a man I could follow round the world!'
But Effie it was — you know, Effie was very shrewd —
Effie it was said 'you'd be throwing yourself away.
Mark my words' Effie said, 'if you chose to follow *that* man
He'd give you the slip: he's not to be trusted.
That man is hollow'. That's what she said.
Or did she say 'yellow'? I'm not quite sure.
You do remember now, don't you, Richard?

LORD CLAVERTON. Not the conversation you have just repeated.
That is new to me. But I do remember you.

MRS. CARGHILL. Time has wrought sad changes in me, Richard.
I was very lovely once. So *you* thought,
And others thought so too. But as you remember,
Please, Richard, just repeat my name — just once:
The name by which you knew me. It would give me such a thrill

    To hear you speak my name once more.

LORD CLAVERTON.   Your name was Maisie Batterson.

MRS. CARGHILL. Oh, Richard, you're only saying that to tease me.
    You know I meant my stage name. The name by which you knew
      me.

LORD CLAVERTON. Well, then, Maisie Montjoy.

MRS. CARGHILL.   Yes. Maisie Montjoy.
    I was Maisie Montjoy once. And you didn't recognise me.

LORD CLAVERTON. You've changed your name, no doubt. And I've
      changed mine.
    Your name now and here . . .

MRS. CARGHILL.   Is Mrs. John Carghill.

LORD CLAVERTON. You married, I suppose, many years ago?

MRS. CARGHILL. Many years ago, the first time. That didn't last long.
    People sometimes say: 'Make one mistake in love,
    You're more than likely to make another'.
    How true that is! Algy was a weakling,
    But simple he was — not sly and slippery.
    Then I married Mr. Carghill. Twenty years older
    Than me, he was. Just what I needed.

LORD CLAVERTON. Is he still living?

MRS. CARGHILL.   He had a weak heart.
    And he worked too hard. Have you never heard
    Of Carghill Equipments? They make office furniture.

LORD CLAVERTON. I've never had to deal with questions of equipment.
    I trust that the business was very successful . . .
    I mean, that he left you comfortably provided for?

MRS. CARGHILL. Well, Richard, my doctor could hardly have sent me
    here
    If I wasn't well off. Yes, I'm provided for.
    But isn't it strange that you and I
    Should meet here at last? Here, of all places!

LORD CLAVERTON. Why not, of all places? What I don't understand
    Is why you should take the first opportunity,
    Finding me here, to revive old memories
    Which I should have thought we both preferred to leave buried.

MRS. CARGHILL. There you're wrong, Richard. Effie always said —
    What a clever girl she was! — 'he doesn't understand women.
    Any woman who trusted *him* would soon find that out'.
    A man may prefer to forget all the women

He has loved. But a woman doesn't want to forget
A single one of her admirers. Why, even a faithless lover
Is still, in her memory, a kind of testimonial.
Men live by forgetting — women live on memories.
Besides a woman has nothing to be ashamed of:
A man is always trying to forget
His own shabby behaviour.

LORD CLAVERTON.   But we'd settled our account.
What harm was done? I learned my lesson
And you learned yours, if you needed the lesson.

MRS. CARGHILL. You refuse to believe that I was really in love with
    you!
Well, it's natural that you shouldn't want to believe it.
But you think, or try to think, that if I'd really suffered
I shouldn't want to let you know who I am,
I shouldn't want to come and talk about the past.
You're wrong, you know. It's both pain and pleasure
To talk about the past — about you and me.
These memories are painful — but I cherish them.

LORD CLAVERTON. If you had really been broken-hearted
I can't see how you could have acted as you did.

MRS. CARGHILL. Who can say whether a heart's been broken
Once it's been repaired? But I know what you mean.
You mean that I would never have started an action
For breach of promise, if I'd really cared for you.
What sentimental nonsense! One starts an action
Simply because one must do *something*.
Well, perhaps I shouldn't have settled out of court.
My lawyer said: 'I advise you to accept',
'Because Mr. Ferry will be standing for Parliament:
His father has political ambitions for him.
If he's lost a breach of promise suit
Some people won't want to appear as his supporters.'
He said: 'What his lawyers are offering in settlement
Is twice as much as I think you'd be awarded.'
Effie was against it — she wanted you exposed.
But I gave way. I didn't want to ruin you.
If I'd carried on, it might have ended your career,
And then you wouldn't have become Lord Claverton.
So perhaps I laid the foundation of your fortunes!

LORD CLAVERTON. And perhaps at the same time of your own?
　　I seem to remember, it was only a year or so
　　Before your name appeared in very large letters
　　In Shaftesbury Avenue.

MRS. CARGHILL. 　　　　　Yes, I had my art.
　　Don't you remember what a hit I made
　　With a number called *It's Not Too Late For You To Love
　　　　Me?*
　　I couldn't have put the feeling into it I did
　　But for what I'd gone through. Did you hear me sing it?

LORD CLAVERTON. Yes, I heard you sing it.

MRS. CARGHILL. 　　　　　　　And what did you feel?

LORD CLAVERTON. Nothing at all. I remember my surprise
　　At finding that I felt nothing at all.
　　I thought, perhaps, what a lucky escape
　　It had been, for both of us.

MRS. CARGHILL. 　　　　That 'both of us'
　　Was an afterthought, Richard. A lucky escape
　　You thought, for you. You felt no embarrassment?

LORD CLAVERTON. Why should I feel embarrassment? My conscience
　　　　was clear.
　　A brief infatuation, ended in the only way possible
　　To our mutual satisfaction.

MRS. CARGHILL. 　　　　　Your conscience was clear.
　　I've very seldom heard people mention their consciences
　　Except to observe that their consciences were clear.
　　You got out of a tangle for a large cash payment
　　And no publicity. So your conscience was clear.
　　At bottom, I believe you're still the same silly Richard
　　You always were. You wanted to pose
　　As a man of the world. And now you're posing
　　As what? I presume, as an elder statesman;
　　And the difference between being an elder statesman
　　And posing successfully as an elder statesman
　　Is practically negligible. And you look the part.
　　Whatever part you've played, I must say you've always looked it.

LORD CLAVERTON. I've no longer any part to play, Maisie.

MRS. CARGHILL. There'll always be some sort of part for you
　　Right to the end. You'll still be playing a part
　　In your obituary, whoever writes it.

LORD CLAVERTON. Considering how long ago it was when you knew
me.
And considering the brevity of our acquaintance,
You're surprisingly confident, I must say,
About your understanding of my character.

MRS. CARGHILL. I've followed your progress year by year, Richard.
And although it's true that our acquaintance was brief,
Our relations were intense enough, I think,
To have given me one or two insights into you.
No, Richard, don't imagine that I'm still in love with you;
And you needn't think I idolise your memory.
It's simply that I feel that we belong together . . .
Now, don't get alarmed. But you touched my soul —
Pawed it, perhaps, and the touch still lingers.
And I've touched yours.
It's frightening to think that we're still together
And more frightening to think that we may *always* be together.
There's a phrase I seem to remember reading somewhere:
Where their fires are not quenched. Do you know what I do?
I read your letters every night.

LORD CLAVERTON. My letters!

MRS. CARGHILL. Have you forgotten that you wrote me letters?
Oh, not very many. Only a few worth keeping.
Only a few. But very beautiful!
It was Effie said, when the break came,
'They'll be worth a fortune to you, Maisie.'
They would have figured at the trial, I suppose,
If there had been a trial. Don't you remember them?

LORD CLAVERTON. Vaguely. Were they very passionate?

MRS. CARGHILL. They were very loving. Would you like to read them?
I'm afraid I can't show you the originals;
They're in my lawyer's safe. But I have photostats
Which are quite as good, I'm told. And I like to read them
In your own handwriting.

LORD CLAVERTON. And have you shown these letters
To many people?

MRS. CARGHILL. Only a few friends.
Effie said: 'If he becomes a famous man
And you should be in want, you could have these letters
auctioned.'

Yes, I'll bring the photostats tomorrow morning,
And read them to you.
                         — Oh, there's Mrs. Piggott!
She's bearing down on us. Isn't she frightful!
She never stops talking. Can you bear it?
If I go at once, perhaps she'll take the hint
And leave us alone tomorrow.
                                        Good morning, Mrs. Piggott!
Isn't it a glorious morning!

[*Enter* MRS. PIGGOTT]

MRS. PIGGOTT. Good morning, Mrs. Carghill!

MRS. CARGHILL.   Dear Mrs. Piggott!
It seems to me that you never sit still:
You simply sacrifice yourself for us.

MRS. PIGGOTT. It's the breath of life to me, Mrs. Carghill,
Attending to my guests. I like to feel they *need* me!

MRS. CARGHILL. You do look after us well, Mrs. Piggott:
You're so considerate — and so understanding.

MRS. PIGGOTT. But I ought to introduce you. You've been talking to
Lord Claverton,
The famous Lord Claverton. This is Mrs. Carghill.
Two of our very nicest guests!
I just came to see that Lord Claverton was comfortable:
We can't allow him to tire himself with talking.
What he needs is *rest*! You're not going, Mrs. Carghill?

MRS. CARGHILL. Oh, I knew that Lord Claverton had come for a rest
cure,
And it struck me that he might find it a strain
To have to cope with both of us at once.
Besides, I ought to do my breathing exercises.

                                                          [*Exit*]

MRS. PIGGOTT. As a matter of fact, I flew to your rescue
(That's why I've brought your morning tipple myself
Instead of leaving it, as usual, to Nurse)
When I saw that Mrs. Carghill had caught you.
You wouldn't know that name, but you might remember her
As Maisie Montjoy in revue.
She was well-known at one time. I'm afraid her name
Means nothing at all to the younger generation,
But you and I should remember her, Lord Claverton.

That tune she was humming, *It's Not Too Late For You To Love
    Me,*
Everybody was singing it once. A charming person,
I dare say, but not quite your sort or mine.
I suspected that she wanted to meet you, so I thought
That I'd take the first opportunity of hinting —
Tactfully, of course — that you should not be disturbed.
Well, she's gone now. If she bothers you again
Just let me know. I'm afraid it's the penalty
Of being famous.
[*Enter* MONICA]
           Oh, Miss Claverton-Ferry!
I didn't see you coming. Now I must fly.

                                  [*Exit*]

MONICA. I saw Mrs. Piggott bothering you again
So I hurried to your rescue. You look tired, Father.
She ought to know better. But I'm all the more distressed
Because I have some . . . not very good news for you.
LORD CLAVERTON. Oh, indeed. What's the matter?
MONICA.   I didn't get far.
I met Michael in the drive. He says he must see you.
I'm afraid that something unpleasant has happened.
LORD CLAVERTON. Was he driving his car?
MONICA.   No, he was walking.
LORD CLAVERTON. I hope he's not had another accident.
You know, after that last escapade of his,
I've lived in terror of his running over somebody.
MONICA. Why, Father, should you be afraid of that?
This shows how bad your nerves have been.
He only ran into a tree.
LORD CLAVERTON.   Yes, a tree.
It might have been a man. But it can't be that,
Or he wouldn't be at large. Perhaps he's in trouble
With some woman or other. I'm sure he has friends
Whom he wouldn't care for you or me to know about.
MONICA. It's probably money.
LORD CLAVERTON.   If it's only debts
Once more, I expect I can put up with it.
But where is he?
MONICA.   I told him he must wait in the garden

Until I had prepared you. I've made him understand
That the doctors want you to be free from worry.
He won't make a scene. But I can see he's frightened.
And you know what Michael is like when he's frightened.
He's apt to be sullen and quick to take offence.
So I hope you'll be patient.

LORD CLAVERTON.   Well then, fetch him.
Let's get this over.

MONICA.   [*calls*] Michael!

[*Enter* MICHAEL]

LORD CLAVERTON.   Good morning, Michael.

MICHAEL. Good morning, Father.

              [*A pause*]

          What a lovely day!
I'm glad you're here, to enjoy such weather.

LORD CLAVERTON. You're glad I'm here? Did you drive down from
     London?

MICHAEL. I drove down last night. I'm staying at a pub
About two miles from here. Not a bad little place.

LORD CLAVERTON. Why are you staying there? I shouldn't have thought
It would be the sort of place that you'd choose for a holiday.

MICHAEL. Well, this isn't a holiday exactly.
But this hotel was very well recommended.
Good cooking, for a country inn. And not at all expensive.

LORD CLAVERTON. You don't normally consider that a
     recommendation.
Are you staying there long? For the whole of this holiday?

MICHAEL. Well, this isn't a holiday, exactly.
Oh. I said that before, didn't I?

MONICA. I wish you'd stop being so polite to each other.
Michael, you know what you've come to ask of Father
And Father knows that you want something from him.
Perhaps you'll get to the point if I leave you together.

                  [*Exit*]

MICHAEL. You know, it's awfully hard to explain things to *you*.
You've always made up your mind that I was to blame
Before you knew the facts. The first thing I remember
Is being blamed for something I hadn't done.
I never got over that. If you always blame a person
It's natural he should end by getting into trouble.

LORD CLAVERTON. You started pretty early getting into trouble,
    When you were expelled from your prep school for stealing.
    But come to the point. You're in trouble again.
    We'll ignore, if you please, the question of blame:
    Which will spare you the necessity of blaming someone else.
    Just tell me what's happened.
MICHAEL.   Well, I've lost my job.
LORD CLAVERTON. The position that Sir Alfred Walter made for you.
MICHAEL. I'd stuck it for two years. And deadly dull it was.
LORD CLAVERTON. Every job is dull, nine-tenths of the time . . .
MICHAEL. I need something much more stimulating.
LORD CLAVERTON.   Well?
MICHAEL. I want to find some more speculative business.
LORD CLAVERTON. I dare say you've tried a little private speculation.
MICHAEL. Several of my friends gave me excellent tips.
    They always came off — the tips I didn't take.
LORD CLAVERTON. And the ones you did take?
MICHAEL.   Not so well, for some reason.
    The fact is, I needed a good deal more capital
    To make anything of it. If I could have borrowed more
    I might have pulled it off.
LORD CLAVERTON.   Borrowed? From whom?
    Not . . . from the firm?
MICHAEL.   I went to a lender,
    A man whom a friend of mine recommended.
    He gave me good terms, on the strength of my name:
    The only good the name has ever done me.
LORD CLAVERTON. On the strength of your name. And what do you
      call good terms?
MICHAEL. I'd nothing at all to pay for two years:
    The interest was just added on to the capital.
LORD CLAVERTON. And how long ago was that?
MICHAEL.   Nearly two years.
    Time passes pretty quickly, when you're in debt.
LORD CLAVERTON. And have you other debts?
MICHAEL.   Oh, ordinary debts:
    My tailor's bill, for instance.
LORD CLAVERTON.   I expected that.
    It was just the same at Oxford.
MICHAEL.   It's their own fault.

They won't send in their bills, and then I forget them.
It's being your son that gets me into debt.
Just because of your name they insist on giving credit.

LORD CLAVERTON. And your debts: are they the cause of your being
    discharged?

MICHAEL. Well, partly. Sir Alfred did come to hear about it,
And so he pretended to be very shocked.
Said he couldn't retain any man on his staff
Who'd taken to gambling. Called me a gambler!
Said he'd communicate with you about it.

LORD CLAVERTON. That accounts for your coming down here so
    precipitately —
In order to let me have your version first.
I dare say Sir Alfred's will be rather different.
And what else did he say?

MICHAEL.   He took the usual line,
Just like the headmaster. And my tutor at Oxford.
'Not what we expected from the son of your father'
And that sort of thing. It's for your sake, he says,
That he wants to keep things quiet. I can tell you, it's no joke
Being the son of a famous public man.
You don't know what I suffered, working in that office.
In the first place, they all knew the job had been made for me
Because I was your son. They considered me superfluous;
They knew I couldn't be living on my pay;
They had a lot of fun with me — sometimes they'd pretend
That I was overworked, when I'd nothing to do.
Even the office boys began to sneer at me.
I wonder I stood it as long as I did.

LORD CLAVERTON. And does this bring us to the end of the list of your
    shortcomings?
Or did Sir Alfred make other unflattering criticisms?

MICHAEL. Well, there was one thing he brought up against me,
That I'd been too familiar with one of the girls.
He assumed it had gone a good deal further than it had.

LORD CLAVERTON. Perhaps it had gone further than you're willing to
    admit.

MICHAEL. Well, after all, she was the only one
Who was at all nice to me. She wasn't exciting,
But it served to pass the time. It would never have happened

If only I'd been given some interesting work!

LORD CLAVERTON. And what do you now propose to do with yourself?

MICHAEL. I want to go abroad.

LORD CLAVERTON.   You want to go abroad?
Well, that's not a bad idea. A few years out of England
In one of the Dominions, might set you on your feet.
I have connections, or at least correspondents
Almost everywhere. Australia — no.
The men I know there are all in the cities:
An outdoor life would suit you better.
How would you like to go to Western Canada?
Or what about sheep farming in New Zealand?

MICHAEL. Sheep farming? Good Lord, no.
That's not my idea. I want to make money.
I want to be somebody on my own account.

LORD CLAVERTON. But what do you want to do? Where do you want
      to go?
What kind of a life do you think you want?

MICHAEL. I simply want to lead a life of my own,
According to my own ideas of good and bad,
Of right and wrong. I want to go far away
To some country where no one has heard the name of Claverton;
Or where, if I took a different name — and I might choose to —
No one would know or care what my name had been.

LORD CLAVERTON. So you are ready to repudiate your family,
To throw away the whole of your inheritance?

MICHAEL. What is my inheritance? As for your title,
I know why you took it. And Mother knew.
First, because it gave you the opportunity
Of retiring from politics, not without dignity,
Being no longer wanted. And you wished to be Lord Claverton
Also, to hold your own with Mother's family —
To lord it over them, in fact. Oh, I've no doubt
That the thought of passing on your name and title
To a son, was gratifying. But it wasn't for *my* sake!
I was just your son — that is to say,
A kind of prolongation of your existence,
A representative carrying on business in your absence.
Why should I thank you for imposing this upon me?
And what satisfaction, I wonder, will it give you

In the grave? If you're still conscious after death,
I bet it will be a surprised state of consciousness.
Poor ghost! reckoning up its profit and loss
And wondering why it bothered about such trifles.

LORD CLAVERTON. So you want me to help you to escape from your
father!

MICHAEL. And to help my father to be rid of *me*.
You simply don't know how very much pleasanter
You will find life become, once I'm out of the country.
What I'd like is a chance to go abroad
As a partner in some interesting business.
But I might be expected to put up some capital.

LORD CLAVERTON. What sort of business have you in mind?

MICHAEL. Oh, I don't know. Import and export,
With an opportunity of profits both ways.

LORD CLAVERTON. This is what I will do for you, Michael.
I will help you to make a start in any business
You may find for yourself — if, on investigation,
I am satisfied about the nature of the business.

MICHAEL. Anyway, I'm determined to get out of England.

LORD CLAVERTON. Michael! Are there reasons for your wanting to go
Beyond what you've told me? It isn't . . . manslaughter?

MICHAEL. Manslaughter? Why manslaughter? Oh, you mean on the
road.
Certainly not. I'm far too good a driver.

LORD CLAVERTON. What then? That young woman?

MICHAEL.   I'm not such a fool
As to get myself involved in a breach of promise suit
Or somebody's divorce. No, you needn't worry
About that girl — or any other.
But I want to get out. I'm fed up with England.

LORD CLAVERTON. I'm sure you don't mean that. But it's natural
enough
To want a few years abroad. It might be very good for you
To find your feet. But I shouldn't like to think
That what inspired you was no positive ambition
But only the desire to escape.

MICHAEL.   I'm not a fugitive.

LORD CLAVERTON. No, not a fugitive from justice —
Only a fugitive from reality.

Oh Michael! If you had some aim of high achievement,
Some dream of excellence, how gladly would I help you!
Even though it carried you away from me forever
To suffer the monotonous sun of the tropics
Or shiver in the northern night. Believe me, Michael:
Those who flee from their past will always lose the race.
I know this from experience. When you reach your goal,
Your imagined paradise of success and grandeur,
You will find your past failures waiting there to greet you.
You're all I have to live for, Michael —
You and Monica. If I lived for twenty years
Knowing that my son had played the coward —
I should merely be another twenty years in dying.

MICHAEL. Very well: if you like, call me a coward.
I wonder whether you would play the hero
If you were in my place. I don't believe you would.
You didn't suffer from the handicap that I've had.
Your father was rich, but was no one in particular,
So you'd nothing to live up to. Those standards of conduct
You've always made so much of, for my benefit:
I wonder whether *you* have always lived up to them.

[MONICA *has entered unobserved*]

MONICA. Michael! How can you speak to Father like that?
Father! What has happened? Why do you look so angry?
I know that Michael must be in great trouble,
So can't you help him?

LORD CLAVERTON.   I am trying to help him,
And to meet him half way. I have made him an offer
Which he must think over. But if he goes abroad
I want him to go in a very different spirit
From that which he has just been exhibiting.

MONICA. Michael! Say something.

MICHAEL.   What is there to say?
I want to leave England, and make my own career:
And Father simply calls me a coward.

MONICA. Father! You know that I would give my life for you.
Oh, how silly that phrase sounds! But there's no vocabulary
For love within a family, love that's lived in
But not looked at, love within the light of which
All else is seen, the love within which

All other love finds speech.
This love is silent.
                    What can I say to you?
However Michael has behaved, Father,
Whatever Father has said, Michael,
You must forgive each other, you must love each other.

MICHAEL. I could have loved Father, if he'd wanted love,
But he never did, Monica, not from me.
You know I've always been very fond of you —
I've a very affectionate nature, really,
But . . .

[*Enter* MRS. CARGHILL *with despatch-case*]

MRS. CARGHILL. Richard! I didn't think you'd still be here.
I came back to have a quiet read of your letters;
But how nice to find a little family party!
I know who you are! You're Monica, of course:
And this must be your brother, Michael.
I'm right, aren't I?

MICHAEL.   Yes, you're right.
But . . .

MRS. CARGHILL. How did I know? Because you're so like your father
When he was your age. He's the picture of you, Richard,
As you were once. You're not to introduce us,
I'll introduce myself. I'm Maisie Montjoy!
That means nothing to you, my dears.
It's a very long time since the name of Maisie Montjoy
Topped the bill in revue. Now I'm Mrs. John Carghill.
Richard! It's astonishing about your children:
Monica hardly resembles you at all,
But Michael — your father has changed a good deal
Since I knew him ever so many years ago,
Yet you're the image of what he was then.
Your father was a very dear friend of mine once.

MICHAEL. Did he really look like me?

MRS. CARGHILL. You've his voice! and his way of moving! It's
                  marvellous.
And the charm! He's inherited all of your charm, Richard.
There's no denying it. But who's this coming?
It's another new guest here. He's waving to us.
Do you know him, Richard?

LORD CLAVERTON.   It's a man I used to know.

MRS. CARGHILL. How interesting! He's a very good figure
    And he's rather exotic-looking. Is he a foreigner?

LORD CLAVERTON. He comes from some place in Central
      America.

MRS. CARGHILL. How romantic! I'd love to meet him.
    He's coming to speak to us. You must introduce him.

[*Enter* GOMEZ]

GOMEZ. Good morning, Dick.

LORD CLAVERTON.   Good morning, Fred.

GOMEZ. You weren't expecting me to join you here, were you?
    You're here for a rest cure. I persuaded my doctor
    That I was in need of a rest cure too.
    And when I heard you'd chosen to come to Badgley Court
    I said to my doctor, 'Well, what about it?
    What better recommendation could I have?'
    So he sent me here.

MRS. CARGHILL.   Oh, you've seen each other lately?
    Richard, I think that you might introduce us.

LORD CLAVERTON. Oh. This is . . .

GOMEZ.   Your old friend Federico Gomez,
    The prominent citizen of San Marco.
    That's my name.

LORD CLAVERTON.   So let me introduce you — by that name —
    To Mrs. . . . Mrs. . . .

MRS. CARGHILL.   Mrs. John Carghill.

GOMEZ. We seem a bit weak on the surnames, Dick!

MRS. CARGHILL. Well, you see, Señor Gomez, when we first became
      friends —
    Lord Claverton and I — I was known by my stage name.
    There was a time, once, when everyone in London
    Knew the name of Maisie Montjoy in revue.

GOMEZ. If Maisie Montjoy was as beautiful to look at
    As Mrs. Carghill, I can well understand
    Her success on the stage.

MRS. CARGHILL.   Oh, did you never see me?
    That's a pity, Señor Gomez.

GOMEZ.   I lost touch with things in England.
    Had I been in London, and in Dick's position
    I should have been your most devoted admirer.

MRS. CARGHILL. *It's Not Too Late For You To Love Me!* That's the song
    That made my reputation, Señor Gomez.

GOMEZ. It will never be too late. Don't you agree, Dick?
    — This young lady I take to be your daughter?
    And this is your son?

LORD CLAVERTON.   This is my son Michael,
    And my daughter Monica.

MONICA.   How do you do.
    Michael!

MICHAEL.   How do you do.

MRS. CARGHILL. I don't believe you've known Lord Claverton
    As long as I have, Señor Gomez.

GOMEZ. My dear lady, you're not old enough
    To have known Dick Ferry as long as I have.
    We were friends at Oxford.

MRS. CARGHILL.   Oh, so you were at Oxford!
    Is that how you come to speak such perfect English?
    Of course, I could tell from your looks that you were Spanish.
    I do like Spaniards. They're so aristocratic.
    But it's very strange that we never met before.
    You were a friend of Richard's at Oxford
    And Richard and I became great friends
    Not long afterwards, didn't we, Richard?

GOMEZ. I expect that was after I had left England.

MRS. CARGHILL. Of course, that explains it. After Oxford
    I suppose you went back to . . . where is your home?

GOMEZ. The republic of San Marco.

MRS. CARGHILL.   Went back to San Marco.
    Señor Gomez, if it's true you're staying at Badgley Court,
    I warn you — I'm going to cross-examine you
    And make you tell me all about Richard
    In his Oxford days.

GOMEZ.   On one condition:
    That you tell me all about Dick when you knew him.

MRS. CARGHILL [*pats her despatch-case*]. Secret for secret, Señor Gomez!
    You've got to be the first to put your cards on the table!

MONICA. Father, I think you should take your rest now.
    — I must explain that the doctors were very insistent

    That my father should rest and have absolute quiet
    Before every meal.

LORD CLAVERTON.   But Michael and I
    Must continue our discussion. This afternoon, Michael.

MONICA. No, I think you've had enough talk for to-day.
    Michael, as you're staying so close at hand
    Will you come back in the morning? After breakfast?

LORD CLAVERTON. Yes, come tomorrow morning.

MICHAEL.   Well, I'll come tomorrow morning.

MRS. CARGHILL. Are you staying in the neighbourhood, Michael?
    Your father is such an old friend of mine
    That it seems most natural to call you Michael.
    You don't mind, do you?

MICHAEL.   No, I don't mind.
    I'm staying at the George — it's not far away.

MRS. CARGHILL. Then I'd like to walk a little way with you.

MICHAEL. Delighted, I'm sure.

GOMEZ.   Taking a holiday?
    You're in business in London, aren't you?

MICHAEL. Not a holiday, no. I've been in business in London,
    But I think of cutting loose, and going abroad.

MRS. CARGHILL. You must tell me all about it. Perhaps I could advise
      you.
    We'll leave you now, Richard. Au revoir, Monica.
    And Señor Gomez, I shall hold you to your promise!

                    [Exeunt MRS. CARGHILL *and* MICHAEL]

GOMEZ. Well, Dick, we've got to obey our doctors' orders.
    But while we're here, we must have some good talks
    About old times. Bye bye for the present.

                              [Exit]

MONICA. Father, those awful people. We mustn't stay here.
    I want you to escape from them.

LORD CLAVERTON.   What I want to escape from
    Is myself, is the past. But what a coward I am,
    To talk of escaping! And what a hypocrite!
    A few minutes ago I was pleading with Michael
    Not to try to escape from his own past failures:
    I said I knew from experience. Do I understand the meaning
    Of the lesson I would teach? Come, I'll start to learn again.
    Michael and I shall go to school together.

We'll sit side by side, at little desks
And suffer the same humiliations
At the hands of the same master. But have I still time?
There is time for Michael. Is it too late for me, Monica?

CURTAIN

Act Three

Same as Act Two. Late afternoon of the following day. MONICA *seated alone. Enter* CHARLES.

CHARLES. Well, Monica, here I am. I hope you got my message.
MONICA. Oh Charles, Charles, Charles, I'm so glad you've come!
    I've been so worried, and rather frightened.
    It was exasperating that they couldn't find me
    When you telephoned this morning. That Mrs. Piggott
    Should have heard my beloved's voice
    And I couldn't, just when I had been yearning
    For the sound of it, for the caress that is in it!
    Oh Charles, how I've wanted you! And now I *need* you.
CHARLES. My darling, what I want is to know that you need me.
    On that last day in London, you admitted that you loved me,
    But I wondered . . . I'm sorry, I couldn't help wondering
    How much your words meant. You didn't seem to need me then.
    And you said we weren't engaged yet . . .
MONICA.   We're engaged now.
    At least *I'm* engaged. I'm engaged to you for ever.
CHARLES. There's another shopping expedition we must make!
    But my darling, since I got your letter this morning
    About your father and Michael, and those people from his past,
    I've been trying to think what I could do to help him.
    If it's blackmail, and that's very much what it looks like,
    Do you think I could persuade him to confide in me?
MONICA. Oh Charles! How could anyone blackmail Father?
    Father, of all people the most scrupulous,
    The most austere. It's quite impossible.
    Father with a guilty secret in his past!
    I just can't imagine it.
            [CLAVERTON *has entered unobserved*]
MONICA. I never expected you from *that* direction, Father!
    I thought you were indoors. Where have you been?

LORD CLAVERTON. Not far away. Standing under the great beech tree.

MONICA. Why under the beech tree?

LORD CLAVERTON.   I feel drawn to that spot.
    No matter. I heard what you said about guilty secrets.
    There are many things not crimes, Monica,
    Beyond anything of which the law takes cognisance:
    Temporary failures, irreflective aberrations,
    Reckless surrenders, unexplainable impulses,
    Moments we regret in the very next moment,
    Episodes we try to conceal from the world.
    Has there been nothing in your life, Charles Hemington,
    Which you wish to forget? Which you wish to keep unknown?

CHARLES. There are certainly things I would gladly forget, Sir,
    Or rather, which I wish had never happened.
    I can think of things you don't yet know about me, Monica,
    But there's nothing I would ever wish to conceal from you.

LORD CLAVERTON. If there's nothing, truly nothing, that you couldn't
      tell Monica
    Then all is well with you. You're in love with each other —
    I don't need to be told what I've seen for myself!
    And if there is nothing that you conceal from *her*
    However important you may consider it
    To conceal from the rest of the world — your soul is safe.
    If a man has one person, just one in his life,
    To whom he is willing to confess everything —
    And that includes, mind you, not only things criminal,
    Not only turpitude, meanness and cowardice,
    But also situations which are simply ridiculous,
    When he has played the fool (as who has not?) —
    Then he loves that person, and his love will save him.
    I'm afraid that I've never loved anyone, really.
    No, I do love my Monica — but there's the impediment:
    It's impossible to be quite honest with your child
    If you've never been honest with anyone older,
    On terms of equality. To one's child one can't reveal oneself
    While she is a child. And by the time she's grown
    You've woven such a web of fiction about you!
    I've spent my life in trying to forget myself,
    In trying to identify myself with the part
    I had chosen to play. And the longer we pretend

The harder it becomes to drop the pretence,
Walk off the stage, change into our own clothes
And speak as ourselves. So I'd become an idol
To Monica. She worshipped the part I played:
How could I be sure that she would love the actor
If she saw him, off the stage, without his costume and makeup
And without his stage words. Monica!
I've had your love under false pretences.
Now, I'm tired of keeping up those pretences,
But I hope that you'll find a little love in your heart
Still, for your father, when you know him
For what he is, the broken-down actor.

MONICA. I think I should only love you the better, Father,
The more I knew about you. I should understand you better.
There's nothing I'm afraid of learning about Charles,
There's nothing I'm afraid of learning about you.

CHARLES. I was thinking, Sir — forgive the suspicion —
From what Monica has told me about your fellow guests,
Two persons who, she says, claim a very long acquaintance —
I was thinking that if there's any question of blackmail,
I've seen something of it in my practice at the bar.
I'm sure I could help.

MONICA.   Oh Father, do let him.

CHARLES. At least, I think I know the best man to advise you.

LORD CLAVERTON. Blackmail? Yes, I've heard that word before,
Not so very long ago. When I asked him what he wanted.
Oh no, he said, I want nothing from you
Except your friendship and your company.
He's a very rich man. And she's a rich woman.
If people merely blackmail you to get your company
I'm afraid the law can't touch them.

CHARLES.   Then why should you submit?
Why not leave Badgley and escape from them?

LORD CLAVERTON. Because they are not real, Charles. They are merely
ghosts:
Spectres from my past. They've always been with me
Though it was not till lately that I found the living persons
Whose ghosts tormented me, to be only human beings,
Malicious, petty, and I see myself emerging
From my spectral existence into something like reality.

MONICA. But what did the ghosts mean? All these years
    You've kept them to yourself. Did Mother know of them?
LORD CLAVERTON. Your mother knew nothing about them. And I
    know
    That I never knew your mother, as she never knew me.
    I thought that she would never understand
    Or that she would be jealous of the ghosts who haunted me.
    And I'm still of that opinion. How open one's heart
    When one is sure of the wrong response?
    How make a confession with no hope of absolution?
    It was not her fault. We never understood each other.
    And so we lived, with a deep silence between us,
    And she died silently. She had nothing to say to me.
    I think of your mother, when she lay dying:
    Completely without interest in the life that lay behind her
    And completely indifferent to whatever lay ahead of her.
MONICA. It is time to break the silence! Let us share your ghosts!
CHARLES. But these are only human beings, who can be dealt with.
MONICA. Or only ghosts, who can be exorcised!
    Who are they, and what do they stand for in your life?
LORD CLAVERTON. . . . And yet they've both done better for
    themselves
    In consequence of it all. He admitted as much,
    Fred Culverwell . . .
MONICA.   Fred Culverwell?
    Who is Fred Culverwell?
LORD CLAVERTON.   He no longer exists.
    He's Federico Gomez, the Central American,
    A man who's made a fortune by his own peculiar methods,
    A man of great importance and the highest standing
    In his adopted country. He even has sons
    Following in their father's footsteps
    Who are also successful. What would *he* have been
    If he hadn't known me? Only a schoolmaster
    In an obscure grammar school somewhere in the Midlands.
    As for Maisie Batterson . . .
MONICA.   Maisie Batterson?
    Who is Maisie Batterson?
LORD CLAVERTON.   She no longer exists.
    Nor the musical comedy star, Maisie Montjoy.

There is Mrs. John Carghill, the wealthy widow.
But Freddy Culverwell and Maisie Batterson,
And Dick Ferry too, and Richard Ferry —
These are my ghosts. They were people with good in them,
People who might all have been very different
From Gomez, Mrs. Carghill and Lord Claverton.
Freddy admired me, when we were at Oxford;
What did I make of his admiration?
I led him to acquire tastes beyond his means:
So he became a forger. And so he served his term.
Was I responsible for that weakness in him?
Yes, I was.
How easily we ignore the fact that those who admire us
Will imitate our vices as well as our virtues —
Or whatever the qualities for which they did admire us!
And that again may nourish the faults that they were born with.
And Maisie loved me, with whatever capacity
For loving she had — self-centred and foolish —
But we should respect love always when we meet it; .
Even when it's vain and selfish, we must not abuse it.
That is where I failed. And the memory frets me.

CHARLES. But all the same, these two people mustn't persecute you.
We can't allow that. What hold have they upon you?

LORD CLAVERTON. Only the hold of those who know
Something discreditable, dishonourable . . .

MONICA. Then, Father, you should tell *us* what they already know.
Why should you wish to conceal from those who love you
What is known so well to those who hate you?

LORD CLAVERTON.   I will tell you very briefly
And simply. As for Frederick Culverwell,
He re-enters my life to make himself a reminder
Of one occasion the memory of which
He knows very well, has always haunted me.
I was driving back to Oxford. We had two girls with us.
It was late at night. A secondary road.
I ran over an old man lying in the road
And I did not stop. Then another man ran over him.
A lorry driver. He stopped and was arrested,
But was later discharged. It was definitely shown
That the old man had died a natural death

And had been run over after he was dead.
It was only a corpse that we had run over
So neither of us killed him. But *I* didn't stop.
And all my life I have heard, from time to time,
When I least expected, between waking and sleeping,
A voice that whispered, 'you didn't stop!'
I knew the voice: it was Fred Culverwell's.

MONICA. Poor Father! All your life! And no one to share it with;
I never knew how lonely you were
Or why you were lonely.

CHARLES.   And Mrs. Carghill:
What has she against you?

LORD CLAVERTON.   I was her first lover.
I would have married her — but my father prevented that:
Made it worth while for her not to marry me —
That was his way of putting it — and of course
Made it worth while for me not to marry her.
In fact, we were wholly unsuited to each other,
Yet she had a peculiar physical attraction
Which no other woman has had. And she knows it.
And she knows that the ghost of the man I was
Still clings to the ghost of the woman who was Maisie.
We should have been poor, we should certainly have quarrelled,
We should have been unhappy, might have come to divorce;
But she hasn't forgotten or forgiven me.

CHARLES. This man, and this woman, who are so vindictive:
Don't you see that they were as much at fault as you
And that they know it? That's why they are inspired
With revenge — it's their means of self-justification.
Let them tell their versions of their miserable stories,
Confide them in whispers. They cannot harm you.

LORD CLAVERTON. Your reasoning's sound enough. But it's
            irrelevant.
Each of them remembers an occasion
On which I ran away. Very well.
I shan't run away now — run away from *them*.
                        ing that I shall at last escape them.
                        ession to you, Monica:
                        ken towards my freedom,
                        important. I know what you think.

You think that I suffer from a morbid conscience,
From brooding over faults I might well have forgotten.
You think that I'm sickening, when I'm just recovering!
It's hard to make other people realise
The magnitude of things that appear to them petty;
It's harder to confess the sin that no one believes in
Than the crime that everyone can appreciate.
For the crime is in relation to the law
And the sin is in relation to the sinner.
What has made the difference in the last five minutes
Is not the heinousness of my misdeeds
But the fact of my confession. And to you, Monica,
To you, of all people.

CHARLES.   I grant you all that.
But what do you propose? How long, Lord Claverton,
Will you stay here and endure this persecution?

LORD CLAVERTON. To the end. The place and time of liberation
Are, I think, determined. Let us say no more about it.
Meanwhile, I feel sure they are conspiring against me.
I see Mrs. Carghill coming.

MONICA.   Let us go.

LORD CLAVERTON. We will stay here. Let her join us.

[*Enter* MRS. CARGHILL]

MRS. CARGHILL. I've been hunting high and low for you, Richard!
I've some very exciting news for you!
But I suspect . . . Dare I? Yes, I'm sure of it, Monica!
I can tell by the change in your expression to-day;
This must be your fiancé. Do introduce him.

MONICA. Mr. Charles Hemington. Mrs. Carghill.

CHARLES. How do you do.

MRS. CARGHILL.   What a charming name!

CHARLES. I'm glad my name meets with your approval, Mrs. Carghill.

MRS. CARGHILL. And let me congratulate *you*, Mr. Hemington.
You're a very lucky man, to get a girl like Monica.
I take a great interest in her future.
Fancy! I've only known her two days!
But I feel like a mother to her already.
You may say that I just missed being her mother!
I've known her father for a very long time,
And there was a moment when I almost married him,

Oh so long ago. So you see, Mr. Hemington,
I've come to regard her as my adopted daughter.
So much so, that it seems odd to call you Mr. Hemington:
I'm going to call you Charles!

CHARLES.   As you please, Mrs. Carghill.

LORD CLAVERTON. You said you had some exciting news for us.
Would you care to impart it?

MRS. CARGHILL.   It's about dear Michael.

LORD CLAVERTON. Oh? What about Michael?

MRS. CARGHILL.   He's told me all his story.
You've cruelly misunderstood him, Richard.
How he must have suffered! So I put on my thinking cap.
I know you've always thought me utterly brainless,
But I have an idea or two, now and then.
And in the end I discovered what Michael really wanted
For making a new start. He wants to go abroad!
And find his own way in the world. That's very natural.
So I thought, why not appeal to Señor Gomez?
He's a wealthy man, and very important
In his own country. And a friend of Michael's father!
And I found him only too ready to help.

LORD CLAVERTON. And what was Señor Gomez able to suggest?

MRS. CARGHILL. Ah! That's the surprise for which I've come to
          prepare you.
Dear Michael is so happy — all his problems are solved;
And he was so perplexed, poor lamb. Let's all rejoice together.

[*Enter* GOMEZ *and* MICHAEL]

LORD CLAVERTON. Well, Michael, you know I expected you this
          morning,
But you never came.

MICHAEL.   No, Father. I'll explain why.

LORD CLAVERTON. And I learn that you have discussed your problems
With Mrs. Carghill and then with Señor Gomez.

MICHAEL. When I spoke, Father, of my wish to get abroad,
You couldn't see my point of view. What's the use of chasing
Half round the world, for the same sort of job
You got me here in London? With another Sir Alfred
Who'd constitute himself custodian of my morals
And send you back reports. Some sort of place
Where everyone would sneer at the fellow from London,

The limey remittance man for whom a job was made.
No! I want to go where I can make my own way,
Not merely be your son. That's what Señor Gomez sees.
He understands my point of view, if *you* don't.
And he's offered me a job which is just what I wanted.

LORD CLAVERTON. Yes, I see the advantage of a job created for you
By Señor Gomez . . .

MICHAEL.   It's not created for me.
Señor Gomez came to London to find a man to fill it,
And he thinks I'm just the man.

GOMEZ.   Yes, wasn't it extraordinary.

LORD CLAVERTON. Of course you're just the man that Señor Gomez
wants,
But in a different sense, and for different reasons
From what you think. Let me tell you about Gomez.
He's unlikely to try to be custodian of your morals;
His real name is Culverwell . . .

GOMEZ.   My dear Dick,
You're wasting your time, rehearsing ancient history.
Michael knows it already. I've told him myself.
I thought he'd better learn the facts from me
Before he heard your distorted version.
But, Dick, I was nettled by that insinuation
About my not being custodian of Michael's morals.
That is just what I should be! And most appropriate,
Isn't it, Dick, when we recall
That you were once custodian of *my* morals:
Though of course you went a little *faster* than I did.

LORD CLAVERTON. On that point, Fred, you're wasting *your* time:
My daughter and my future son-in-law
Understand that allusion. I have told them the story
In explanation of our . . . intimacy
Which they found puzzling.

MRS. CARGHILL.   Oh, Richard!
Have you explained to them our intimacy too?

LORD CLAVERTON. I have indeed.

MRS. CARGHILL.   The romance of my life.
Your father was simply *irresistible*
In those days. I melted the first time he looked at me!
Some day, Monica, I'll tell you all about it.

MONICA. I am satisfied with what I know already, Mrs. Carghill,
    About you.

MRS. CARGHILL. But I was very lovely then.

GOMEZ. We are sure of that! You're so lovely now
    That we can well imagine you at . . . what age were you?

MRS. CARGHILL. Just eighteen.

LORD CLAVERTON.   Now, Michael,
    Señor Gomez says he has told you his story.
    Did he include the fact that he served a term in prison?

MICHAEL. He told me everything. It was his experience
    With you, that made him so understanding
    Of my predicament.

LORD CLAVERTON.   And made him invent
    The position which he'd come to find the man for.

MICHAEL. I don't care about that. He's offered me the job
    With a jolly good screw, and some pickings in commissions.
    He's made a fortune there. San Marco for me!

LORD CLAVERTON. And what are your duties to be? Do you know?

MICHAEL. We didn't go into details. There's time for that later.

GOMEZ. Much better to wait until we get there.
    The nature of business in San Marco
    Is easier explained in San Marco than in England.

LORD CLAVERTON. Perhaps you intend to change your name to
        Gomez?

GOMEZ. Oh no, Dick, there are plenty of other good names.

MONICA. Michael ,Michael, you can't abandon your family
    And your very self — it's a kind of suicide.

CHARLES. Michael, you think Señor Gomez is inspired by
        benevolence —

MICHAEL. I told you he'd come to London looking for a man
    For an important post on his staff —

CHARLES. A post the nature of which is left very vague

MICHAEL. It's confidential, I tell you.

CHARLES.   So I can imagine:
    Highly confidential . . .

GOMEZ.   Be careful, Mr. Barrister.
    You ought to know something about the law of slander.
    Here's Mrs. Carghill, a reliable witness.

CHARLES. I know enough about the law of libel and slander
    To know that you are hardly likely to invoke it.

And, Michael, here's another point to think of:
Señor Gomez has offered you a post in San Marco,
Señor Gomez pays your passage . . .

MICHAEL.   And an advance of salary.

CHARLES. Señor Gomez pays your passage . . .

GOMEZ.   Just as many years ago
His father paid mine.

CHARLES.   This return of past kindness
No doubt gives you pleasure?

GOMEZ.   Yes, it's always pleasant
To repay an old debt. And better late than never.

CHARLES. I see your point of view. Can you really feel confidence,
Michael, in a man who aims to gratify, through you,
His lifelong grievance against your father?
Remember, you put yourself completely in the power
Of a man you don't know, of the nature of whose business
You know nothing. All you can be sure of
Is that he served a prison sentence for forgery.

GOMEZ. Well, Michael, what do you say to all this?

MICHAEL. I'll say that Hemington has plenty of cheek.
Señor Gomez and I have talked things over, Hemington . . .

GOMEZ. As two men of the world, we discussed things very frankly;
And I can tell you, Michael's head is well screwed on.
He's got brains, he's got flair. When he does come back
He'll be able to buy you out many times over.

MRS. CARGHILL. Richard, I think it's time *I* joined the conversation.
My late husband, Mr. Carghill, was a business man —
I wish you could have known him, Señor Gomez!
You're very much alike in some ways —
So I understand business. Mr. Carghill told me so.
Now, Michael has great abilities for business.
I saw that, and so does Señor Gomez.
He's simply been suffering, poor boy, from frustration.
He's been waiting all this time for opportunity
To make use of his gifts; and now, opportunity —
Opportunity has come knocking at the door.
Richard, you must not bar his way. That would be shameful.

LORD CLAVERTON. I cannot bar his way, as you know very well.
Michael's a free agent. So if he chooses
To place himself in your power, Fred Culverwell,

64

Of his own volition to contract his enslavement,
I cannot prevent him. I have something to say to you,
Michael, before you go. I shall never repudiate you
Though you repudiate me. I see now clearly
The many many mistakes I have made
My whole life through, mistake upon mistake,
The mistaken attempts to correct mistakes
By methods which proved to be equally mistaken.
I see that your mother and I, in our failure
To understand each other, both misunderstood you
In our divergent ways. When I think of your childhood,
When I think of the happy little boy who was Michael,
When I think of your boyhood and adolescence,
And see how all the efforts aimed at your good
Only succeeded in defeating each other,
How can I feel anything but sorrow and compunction?

MONICA. Oh Michael, remember, you're my only brother
And I'm your only sister. You never took much notice of me.
When we were growing up we seldom had the same friends.
I took all that for granted. So I didn't know till now
How much it means to me to have a brother.

MICHAEL. Why of course, Monica. You know I'm very fond of you
Though we never really seemed to have much in common.
I remember, when I came home for the holidays
How it used to get on my nerves, when I saw you
Always sitting there with your nose in a book.
And once, Mother snatched a book away from you
And tossed it into the fire. How I laughed!
You never seemed even to want a flirtation,
And my friends used to chaff me about my highbrow sister.
But all the same, I was fond of you, and always shall be.
We don't meet often, but if we're fond of each other,
That needn't interfere with your life or mine.

MONICA. Oh Michael, you haven't understood a single word
Of what I said. You must make your own life
Of course, just as I must make mine.
It's not a question of your going abroad
But a question of the spirit which inspired your decision:
If you wish to renounce your father and your family
What is left between you and me?

MICHAEL. That makes no difference.
You'll be seeing me again.

MONICA. But who will you be
When I see you again? Whoever you are then
I shall always pretend that it is the same Michael.

CHARLES. And when do you leave England?

MICHAEL. When we can get a passage.
And I must buy my kit. We're just going up to London.
Señor Gomez will attend to my needs for that climate.
And you see, he has friends in the shipping line
Who he thinks can be helpful in getting reservations.

MRS. CARGHILL. It's wonderful, Señor Gomez, how you manage
everything!
— No sooner had I put my proposal before him
Than he had it all planned out! It really was an inspiration —
On my part, I mean. Are you listening to me, Richard?
You look very *distrait*. You ought to be excited!

LORD CLAVERTON. Is this good-bye then, Michael?

MICHAEL. Well, that just depends.
I could look in again. If there's any point in it.
Personally, I think that when one's come to a decision,
It's as well to say good-bye at once and be done with it.

LORD CLAVERTON. Yes, if you're going, and I see no way to stop you,
Then I agree with you, the sooner the better.
We may never meet again, Michael.

MICHAEL. I don't see why not.

GOMEZ. At the end of five years he will get his first leave.

MICHAEL. Well . . . there's nothing more to say, is there?

LORD CLAVERTON. Nothing at all.

MICHAEL. Then we might as well be going.

GOMEZ. Yes, we might as well be going.
You'll be grateful to me in the end, Dick.

MRS. CARGHILL. A parent isn't always the right person, Richard,
To solve a son's problems. Sometimes an outsider,
A friend of the family, can see more clearly.

GOMEZ. Not that I deserve any credit for it.
We can only regard it as a stroke of good fortune
That I came to England at the very moment
When I could be helpful.

MRS. CARGHILL. It's truly providential!

MONICA. Good-bye Michael. Will you let me write to you?

GOMEZ. Oh, I'm glad you reminded me. Here's my business card
With the full address. You can always reach him there.
But it takes some days, you know, even by air mail.

MONICA. Take the card, Charles. If I write to you, Michael,
Will you ever answer?

MICHAEL.　　　　　Oh of course, Monica.
You know I'm not much of a correspondent;
But I'll send you a card, now and again,
Just to let you know I'm flourishing.

LORD CLAVERTON.　　　　　Yes, write to Monica.

GOMEZ. Well, good-bye Dick. And good-bye Monica.
Good-bye, Mr. . . . Hemington.

MONICA.　　　　　Good-bye Michael.

　　　　　　　　　　[*Exeunt* MICHAEL *and* GOMEZ]

MRS. CARGHILL. I'm afraid this seems awfully sudden to you,
　　　Richard;
It isn't so sudden. We talked it all over.
But I've got a little piece of news of my own:
Next autumn, I'm going out to Australia,
On my doctor's advice. And on my way back
Señor Gomez has invited me to visit San Marco.
I'm so excited! But what pleases me most
Is that I shall be able to bring you news of Michael.
And now that we've found each other again,
We must always keep in touch. But you'd better rest now.
You're looking rather tired. I'll run and see them off.

　　　　　　　　　　[*Exit* MRS. CARGHILL]

MONICA. Oh Father, Father, I'm so sorry!
But perhaps, perhaps, Michael may learn his lesson.
I believe he'll come back. If it's all a failure
Homesickness, I'm sure, will bring him back to us;
If he prospers, that will give him confidence —
It's only self-confidence that Michael is lacking.
Oh Father, it's not you and me he rejects,
But himself, the unhappy self that he's ashamed of.
I'm sure he loves us.

LORD CLAVERTON.　　　Monica my dear,
What you say comes home to me. I fear for Michael;
Nevertheless, you are right to hope for something better.

And when he comes back, if he does come back,
I know that you and Charles will do what you can
To make him feel that he is not estranged from you.

CHARLES. We will indeed. We shall be ready to welcome him
And give all the aid we can. But it's both of you together
Make the force to attract him: you and Monica combined.

LORD CLAVERTON. I shall not be here. You heard me say to him
That this might be a final good-bye.
I am sure of it now. Perhaps it is as well.

MONICA. What do you mean, Father? You'll be here to greet him.
But one thing I'm convinced of: you must leave Badgley Court.

CHARLES. Monica is right. You should leave.

LORD CLAVERTON. This may surprise you: I feel at peace now.
It is the peace that ensues upon contrition
When contrition ensues upon knowledge of the truth.
Why did I always want to dominate my children?
Why did I mark out a narrow path for Michael?
Because I wanted to perpetuate myself in him.
Why did I want to keep you to myself, Monica?
Because I wanted you to give your life to adoring
The man that I pretended to myself that I was,
So that I could believe in my own pretences.
I've only just now had the illumination
Of knowing what love is. We all think we know,
But how few of us do! And now I feel happy —
In spite of everything, in defiance of reason,
I have been brushed by the wing of happiness.
And I am happy, Monica, that you have found a man
Whom you can love for the man he really is.

MONICA. Oh Father, I've always loved you,
But I love you more since I have come to know you
Here, at Badgley Court. And I love you the more
Because I love Charles.

LORD CLAVERTON.   Yes, my dear.
Your love is for the real Charles, not a make-believe,
As was your love for me.

MONICA.   But not now, Father!
It's the real you I love — the man you are,
Not the man I thought you were.

LORD CLAVERTON.   And Michael —

I love him, even for rejecting me,
For the *me* he rejected, I reject also.
I've been freed from the self that pretends to be someone;
And in becoming no one, I begin to live.
It is worth while dying, to find out what life is.
And I love you, my daughter, the more truly for knowing
That there is someone you love more than your father —
That you love and are loved. And now that I love Michael,
I think, for the first time — remember, my dear,
I am only a beginner in the practice of loving —
Well, that is something.

      I shall leave you for a while.
This is your first visit to us at Badgley Court,
Charles, and not at all what you were expecting.
I am sorry you have had to see so much of persons
And situations not very agreeable.
You two ought to have a little time together.
I leave Monica to you. Look after her, Charles,
Now and always. I shall take a stroll.

MONICA. At this time of day? You'll not go far, will you?
 You know you're not allowed to stop out late
 At this season. It's chilly at dusk.

LORD CLAVERTON. Yes, it's chilly at dusk. But I'll be warm enough.
 I shall not go far.

            [*Exit* CLAVERTON]

CHARLES. He's a very different man from the man he used to be.
 It's as if he had passed through some door unseen by us
 And had turned and was looking back at us
 With a glance of farewell.

MONICA. I can't understand his going for a walk.

CHARLES. He wanted to leave us alone together!

MONICA. Yes, he wanted to leave us alone together.
 And yet, Charles, though we've been alone to-day
 Only a few minutes, I've felt all the time . . .

CHARLES. I know what you're going to say!
 We *were* alone together, in some mysterious fashion,
 Even with Michael, and despite those people,
 Because somehow we'd begun to belong together,
 And that awareness . . .

MONICA. Was a shield protecting both of us . . .

CHARLES. So that now we are conscious of a new person
Who is you and me together.

Oh my dear,
I love you to the limits of speech, and beyond.
It's strange that words are so inadequate.
Yet, like the asthmatic struggling for breath,
So the lover must struggle for words.

MONICA. I've loved you from the beginning of the world.
Before you and I were born, the love was always there
That brought us together.

Oh Father, Father!
I could speak to you now.

CHARLES. Let me go and find him.

MONICA. We will go to him together. He is close at hand,
Though he has gone too far to return to us.
He is under the beech tree. It is quiet and cold there.
In becoming no one, he has become himself.
He is only my father now, and Michael's.
And I am happy. Isn't it strange, Charles,
To be happy at this moment?

CHARLES. It is not at all strange.
The dead has poured out a blessing on the living.

MONICA. Age and decrepitude can have no terrors for me,
Loss and vicissitude cannot appal me,
Not even death can dismay or amaze me
Fixed in the certainty of love unchanging.

I feel utterly secure
In you; I am a part of you. Now take me to my father.

CURTAIN

70